SCHOLASTIC EARLY SCIENCE

Little Snake Plays Hide and Seek

How Animals Hide

Mathangi Subramanian
Illustrated by Suvidha Mistry

For

Ram Subramanian

Mathangi Subramanian is a writer and educator who believes stories have the power to change the world. She has worked in education policy, children's television and teacher preparation, and began her career as a science teacher in Texas and New York City. She currently splits her time between Bangalore and Washington, DC.

Suvidha Mistry is a freelance illustrator with a passion for all forms of art. She loves to tell stories with her illustrations, sketches and photographs. She has worked with multimedia firms as a graphic head and is now living her dream of being an illustrator of children's books.

Published by Scholastic India Pvt. Ltd.
A subsidiary of Scholastic Inc., New York, 10012 (USA).
Publishers since 1920, with international operations in Canada, Australia, New Zealand, the United Kingdom, India, and Hong Kong.

For information regarding permission, write to:
Scholastic India Pvt. Ltd.
A-27, Ground Floor, Bharti Sigma Centre
Infocity-1, Sector 34, Gurgaon 122001 (India)

First edition: December 2014
This reprint edition: June 2026

ISBN-13: 978-93-5103-906-8

Printed in India at Shiv Shakti Printing and Trading Co., Haryana

It was a beautiful afternoon in the forest. Little Snake said, ‘Let’s play a game.’

‘What shall we play?’ asked Squirrel.

‘Hide and seek!’ said Turtle.

‘I know a hiding place where you’ll never find me,’ said Butterfly.

'If we all hide, who will seek?' asked Parakeet. 'I will!' said Little Snake.

'But Little Snake,' said Frog, 'you can't fly or swim or run. How will you find us?'

'I may not be able to fly or swim or run,' said Little Snake, 'but I can certainly find you. Now run and hide!'

The friends flapped and fluttered and scurried and scampered and creeped and crawled away.

Little Snake closed her eyes and said, '1-2-3-4-5-6-7-8-9-10! Ready or not, here I come!'

Little Snake slithered across the forest floor. Her body went shush-shush-shush when she moved.

But when she stopped, she heard it again—shush-shush-shush. It was coming from the spotted, knotted trunk of a tree.

'Why, that's not the bark of the tree at all!' said Little Snake.

'It's Squirrel!'

Squirrel lay flat against the tree so her body looked like bark and her stripes looked like twigs. But she couldn't stop her tail from twitching with a shush-shush-shush.

'You found me!' Squirrel said.

'Come, let's find the others,' said Little Snake.

one

Little Snake and Squirrel came to the river. It was full of rocks. The river made a swish-swish-swish sound.

Little Snake looked at the rocks.

There were ...

two three four five

The fifth rock did not look like the others.
True, it was smooth and shiny and black.
But it was also somehow different.

'Why that's not a rock at all!'
Little Snake said.

'It's Turtle!'

Turtle poked his head out of the water.

'You found me!' Turtle said.

'Come, let's find the others,' said Little Snake.

By the side of the water, Turtle tripped.

'What did you trip over?' asked Squirrel.

'It's just a bunch of junk, plants and shells and pieces of rock,' said Turtle. But Little Snake looked closer.

Underneath the junk, Little Snake saw darting eyes and long, snappy claws.

'Why that's not junk at all!' said Snake.

'It's Crab!'

'You found me!' Crab said.

'Come, let's find the others,' said Little Snake.

The shore was a muddy mix of colours
like green and black and brown.

'It's glippy and gloppy,' said Squirrel.

'It's slippery and sloppy,' said Turtle.

But what was that? Did that glippy, gloppy,
slippery, sloppy mud just move?

'Why that's not mud at all!' said Little Snake.

'It's Frog!'

Frog blinked her big black eyes and hopped out of the mud. 'You found me!' Frog said.

'Come, let's find the others,' said Little Snake.

The friends came to a thick maze of bushes.

'Watch out, Little Snake,' said Squirrel.
'There's something in those bushes!'

Little Snake saw a pair of bright yellow eyes between the leaves.

Squirrel scrambled up a tree.

Frog hopped behind a rock.

Turtle pulled his head and legs into his shell.

But Little Snake looked closer.

'Why those are not eyes at all!' said Little Snake.

'It's Butterfly!'

'You found me!' Butterfly said.

'Come, let's find the others,' said Little Snake.

The friends slithered and scampered and flopped and fluttered out of the mud into a field full of grass.

'No one can hide here,' said Crab.
'There are no rocks to sit under,' said Frog.
'There are no trees to climb up,' said Squirrel.
'There's no water to swim through,' said Turtle.
'Are you sure?' asked Little Snake.

The animals looked closer.

Why was that blade of grass standing straighter than the rest?

'Why that's not grass at all!' said Little Snake.

'It's Grasshopper!'

'You found me!' said Grasshopper.

'Come, let's find the others,' said Little Snake.

The grass cast long shadows on the ground.

'Look at the way the grass ripples in the wind,' said Grasshopper.

Little Snake looked closer. The waving grass and long shadows looked orange and black.

But why did that orange and black shadow have long, fine whiskers?

Animals do not just use camouflage to hide from predators.

'Why that is
not grass at all!'
said Little Snake.

'It's Baby Tiger!'

Baby Tiger came forward on his huge, silent paws. His orange and black stripes looked just like grass waving in the wind.

'You found me!' Baby Tiger said.

'Come, let's find the others,'
said Little Snake.

Little Snake's tongue darted in and out of her mouth, tasting the air.

'Mmmm, something smells like bananas,' said Little Snake.

Little Snake looked up into the branches of the banana trees. The trees swayed and creaked in the wind. Which one held the sweetest bunch?

'It must be that one,' said Little Snake, looking at a bunch of yellow bananas covered with a long, green leaf.

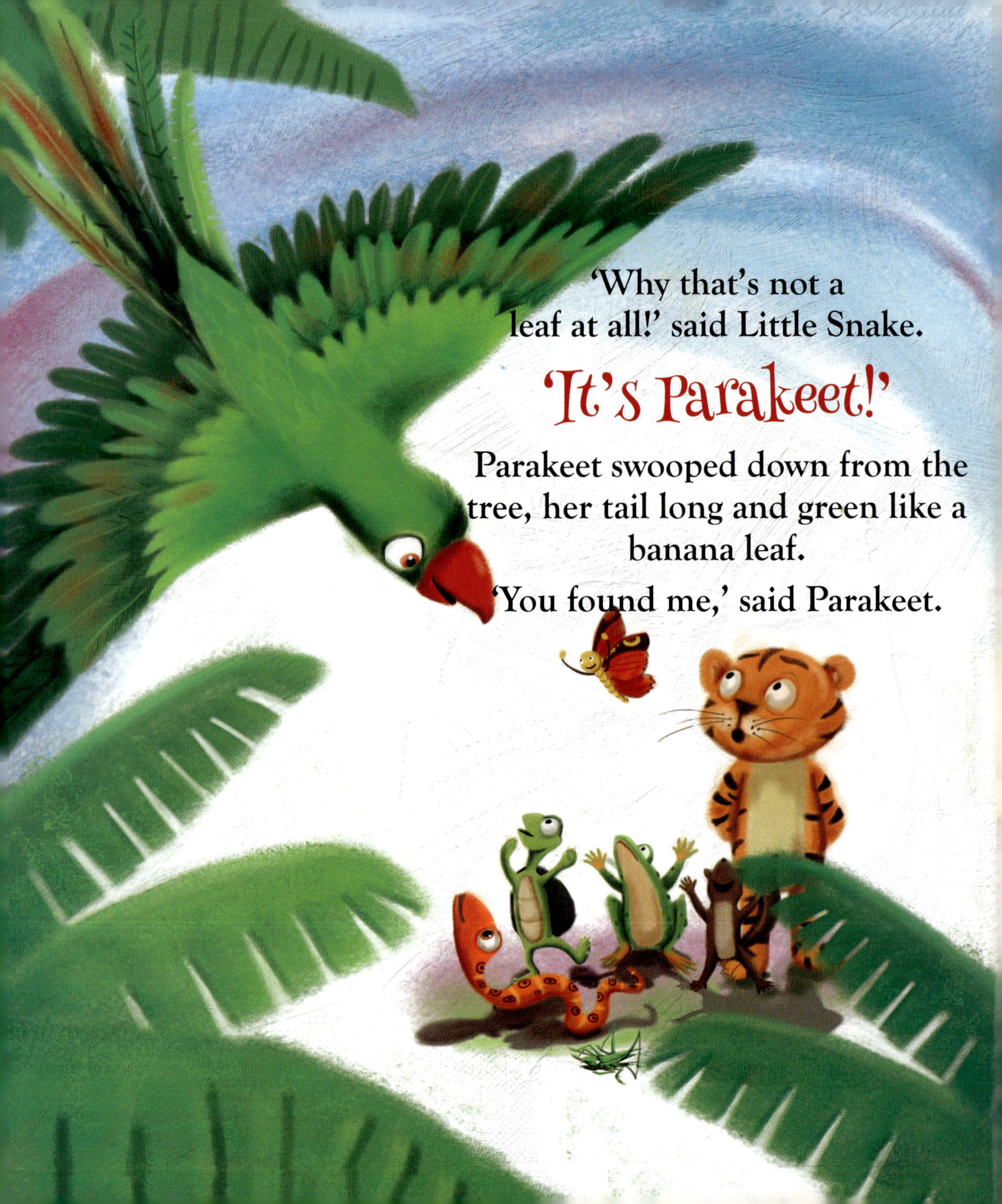

'Why that's not a
leaf at all!' said Little Snake.

'It's Parakeet!'

Parakeet swooped down from the tree, her tail long and green like a banana leaf.

'You found me,' said Parakeet.

'Now there is just one more animal to find!' said Little Snake.

'What do you mean, Little Snake?' asked Butterfly. 'You've found us all!'

But Little Snake was gone!

'Little Snake?' said Squirrel and Turtle and Crab.

'Little Snake?' said Butterfly and Frog and Grasshopper.

'Little Snake?' said Parakeet and Baby Tiger.

'Here I am!' said Little Snake. Her friends turned to the sound coming from the forest floor. Little Snake's spotted, scaly skin blended in perfectly with the pebbles and mud and fallen leaves.

'Wow, Little Snake,' said Squirrel. 'You may not have legs or feathers or fins or feet, but you are the champion of hide and seek.'

'You don't need legs or feathers or fins or feet to play,' said Little Snake. 'All you need is a great big forest and a few good friends.'

FUN FACTS

1. Animals use their **five senses** to explore their worlds.
2. The five senses are **hearing, seeing, smelling, tasting** and **touching**.
3. Snakes smell using their **tongues**.
4. Although snakes do not have visible ears, they have excellent **hearing**.
5. **Camouflage** means hiding by blending in with the world around you.
6. Many animals use camouflage to **protect** themselves from danger.
7. Squirrels have fur that is **brown** and **speckled** like tree bark. This is their camouflage.
8. Another kind of camouflage is **mimesis** or **imitation**, where animals pretend to be other things.
9. When turtles pull their legs and head into their **shells**, they look like rocks. This is an example of mimesis.
10. **Decorator crabs** camouflage themselves by covering their shells with material from their environment.
11. They attach **seaweed**, **rocks** and **gravel** to the backs of their shells.
12. Some animals cover parts of their bodies to **improve** their camouflage.
13. Frogs close their eyes when hiding because their **eyelids** are camouflaged.
14. Another kind of camouflage is **mimicry**, where animals pretend to be something they are not.
15. Some butterflies have wings that look like the eyes of birds of prey, like **owls** or **falcons**.
16. This tricks other animals into thinking that **butterflies** are dangerous.
17. Insects often camouflage themselves as **twigs** or **sticks** or **blades of grass**.
18. Some **grasshoppers** look like grass, while others look like mud or sand.
19. **Hunters** like tigers use camouflage to hide from their prey.
20. Camouflage does not have to be in **dull colours**.
21. In the tropics, brightly coloured animals **blend in** with leaves and flowers.
22. Some baby **snakes** are camouflaged to protect them until they become adults.
23. When they grow up, they get **new skin** that can be brightly coloured.